THE WATERFIRE DUCK

Written by
KIKI LATIMER

Illustrated by
BUNNY GRIFFETH

Author: Kiki Latimer
Illustrator: Bunny Griffeth
Page Layout: Thomas Payne and Laura Duclos
© Copyright 2009, Educa Vision Inc.
Coconut Creek, FL

For information, please contact:

Educa Vision Inc.,
7550 NW 47th Avenue
Coconut Creek, FL 33073
Telephone: 954-968-7433
Fax: 954-970-0330
E-mail: educa@aol.com
Web: www.educavision.com

ISBN 13: 978-1-58432-573-4

Dedicated
to
Barnaby Evans, the creator of WaterFire,
to all who love and share the magic of WaterFire,
to the people of the great city of Providence,
and
to my husband Jim
who was with me when we first saw
the little brown duck.

Special thanks to Barnaby Evans and Don Kirk
for delightful and informative editorial assistance.

It was springtime in the marsh on Narragansett Bay
and Little Duck waited quietly inside her egg.
Outside Mama Duck listened to the songs in the wind
and waited for Little Duck to hatch.

"Rat-a-tat-tat!" Little Duck tapped on the shell.
"Rat-a-tat-tat!" She tapped out the beat. Then she was quiet.
She too listened to the sound of the wind over the bay.

Sometimes soft and high like a flute.
Sometimes gentle like a violin.
Sometimes deep and strong like a cello.

Little Duck listened to the music in the
wind. And then she joined in once again...
"Rat-a-tat-tat! Rat-a-tat-tat-crack!"
Out came Little Duck – a beautiful
golden brown baby mallard!

Little Duck fluffed up her downy feathers
and patted her feet in time with the music
in the wind. She danced and twirled with
a rat-a-tat-tat!

Mama Duck led Little Duck down to the water. "I love that you can dance, now you must learn to listen for your own special song in the wind."

Little Duck twirled and danced with a rat-a-tat-tat!

All that spring, Little Duck ate little bugs and new weeds and grew bigger with a rat-a-tat-tat!

All that spring, Little Duck listened to the wind.

After a while she thought she could hear the beginnings of a song between the notes:

"There's a place where the rivers meet the sea."

Summer came and Little Duck ate fat bugs
and green weeds and grew even bigger with a
rat-a-tat-tat!

All summer long Little Duck listened to the wind.

After a while she thought she could hear the second line
of a song between the notes:

"There's a city that waits for you and me!"

Little Duck hummed these
words over and over
with the wind.

Fall came and it grew cooler. Now Little Duck ate sleepy bugs and
brown weeds, and grew bigger and bigger with a rat-a-tat-tat!

Little Duck listened to the wind as it blew the leaves off trees.

After a while she thought she could hear the third line of a song
between the notes:

"Fires dance on the waters
and music fills the air!"

"Oh my!" thought Little Duck
and she hummed these words
over and over with the wind.

Winter came and she fluffed her feathers to keep
warm. Little Duck ate cold bugs and frozen weeds
and grew bigger still with a rat-a-tat-tat!

All winter long, Little Duck listened to the icy cold wind.

After a while she thought she could hear the last
line of the wind's song:

"Find it, find it, find it –
If you dare!"

Finally, the warm springtime came once again.
Little Duck was now full grown. Rat-a-tat-tat!
She listened carefully to her song in the wind:

"There's a place where the rivers meet the sea.
There's a city that waits for you and me.
Fires dance on the waters
And music fills the air –
Find it, find it, find it –
If you dare!"

Little Duck knew it was time
to follow her song!

She ventured out of the marsh waters
and north into Narragansett Bay.

During the day there was sunlight
and sparkling blue green waters
and little silvery fish to eat.

At night Little Duck watched the moon rise
and the dark night sky glitter overhead with stars.

She sang and her song floated in the wind:

"There's a place where the rivers meet the sea.
There's a city that waits for you and me.
Fires dance on the waters
And music fills the air –
Find it, find it, find it –
If you dare!"

Then Little Duck slept.

Morning came and Little Duck paddled
out into the sunlit bay. Rat-a-tat-tat!

She could see the Jamestown Bridge and
the Newport Bridge. Everywhere there
were sailboats, shiny motorboats,
and huge cruise liners!

And there were seals!

She paddled under the Newport Bridge. It was very big
and Little Duck felt very small.

Just then a small white harp seal pup popped his head up
and he asked, "Where are you going Little Duck?"

"Oh! Hello!" said Little Duck and then she sang her song:

"There's a place where the rivers meet the sea.
There's a city that waits for you and me.
Fires dance on the waters
And music fills the air..."

The little seal rolled his eyes and said,
"Oh my! What a silly little duck!"
and he swam away with a flick of his whiskers.

The next day Little Duck paddled and twirled and danced past Prudence Island. There in the grass was a beautiful soft brown deer. The deer looked up from her grazing and asked "Where are you going Little Duck?"

"Oh! Hello!" said Little Duck and then she sang her song:

"There's a place where the rivers meet the sea.
There's a city that waits for you and me.
Fires dance on the waters
And music fills the air..."

The deer rolled her eyes and said, "Shush! What a silly duck!"
And she turned and strolled away with a flick of her tail.

Little Duck paddled on and she hummed her song quietly.

The next day Little Duck paddled
and paddled on the great big bay.

It began to get dark and she was getting tired.
She hummed her song again very quietly to herself
and wondered if she really was a silly little duck.
She did not rat-a-tat-tat.

She looked up at the dark night sky with its stars beginning to pop out
one by one. The moon was rising and shone on the big sad tear that now
slipped down Little Duck's beak. She felt very far from home.
The night was dark and the wind was silent. Little Duck felt all alone.
Maybe it was time to turn back.

Just then a very old sea turtle swam out from under a big bridge. The old turtle glided along, nodded gently to Little Duck, and quietly hummed a familiar tune.

Little Duck's heart leapt as she recognized her song. The old sea turtle nodded once more to Little Duck and turned out to the bay. Before Little Duck could lose heart, she plunged into the dark waters and paddled under the bridge.

The wind stirred gently across the waters.

Suddenly Little Duck realized that in the dusk she could now see
both sides of the shore. She was where the rivers meet the sea!
Rat-a-tat-tat!

Little Duck paddled up the Providence River. She listened to the wind.
Now there was a new sound on the water and then a wonderful deep
woody smell that made Little Duck sniff the air.
She sniffed and listened very carefully.

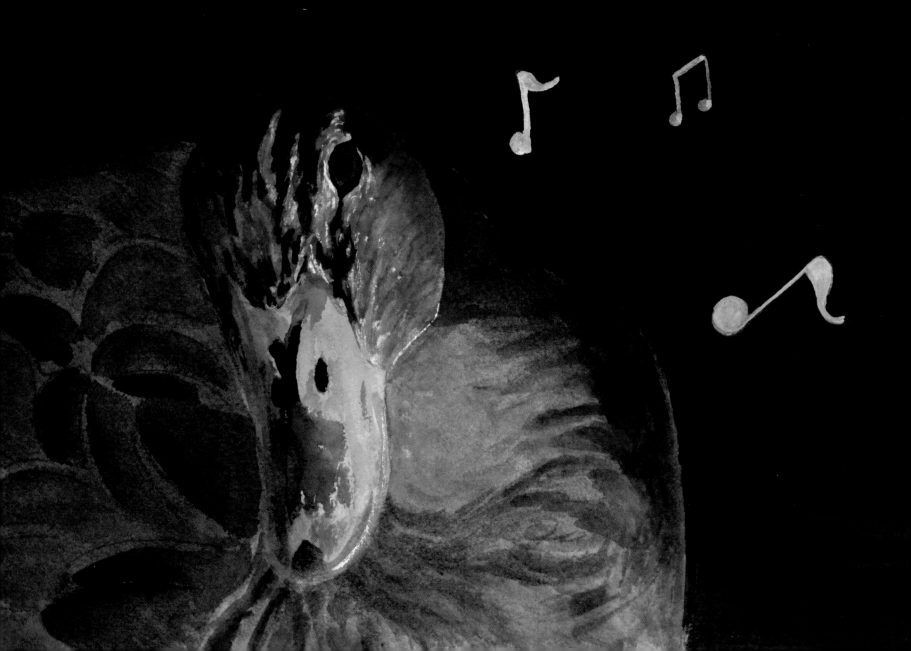

Then Little Duck saw something she had never seen before. There in the middle of the river a large blazing fire danced and leaped and glowed! Yellows, oranges and reds flashed, glittered and rippled across the canvas of the night-black water.

The light caught and played upon the movement of the river. Embers leapt and glowed and sparks waltzed upward into the deep purple night sky to dance with the stars above! Little Duck had never seen such beauty!

She rushed forward to dance and swim and twirl
in the golden reflections flickering on
the dark water.

Rat-a-tat-tat!

And then she saw that there was another fire beyond the first. And then another!
And as she looked up the river she saw one blazing fire after another.
One hundred bonfires all floating above the water!
All surrounded by the notes of flutes,
violins and cellos...and more!
So much more!

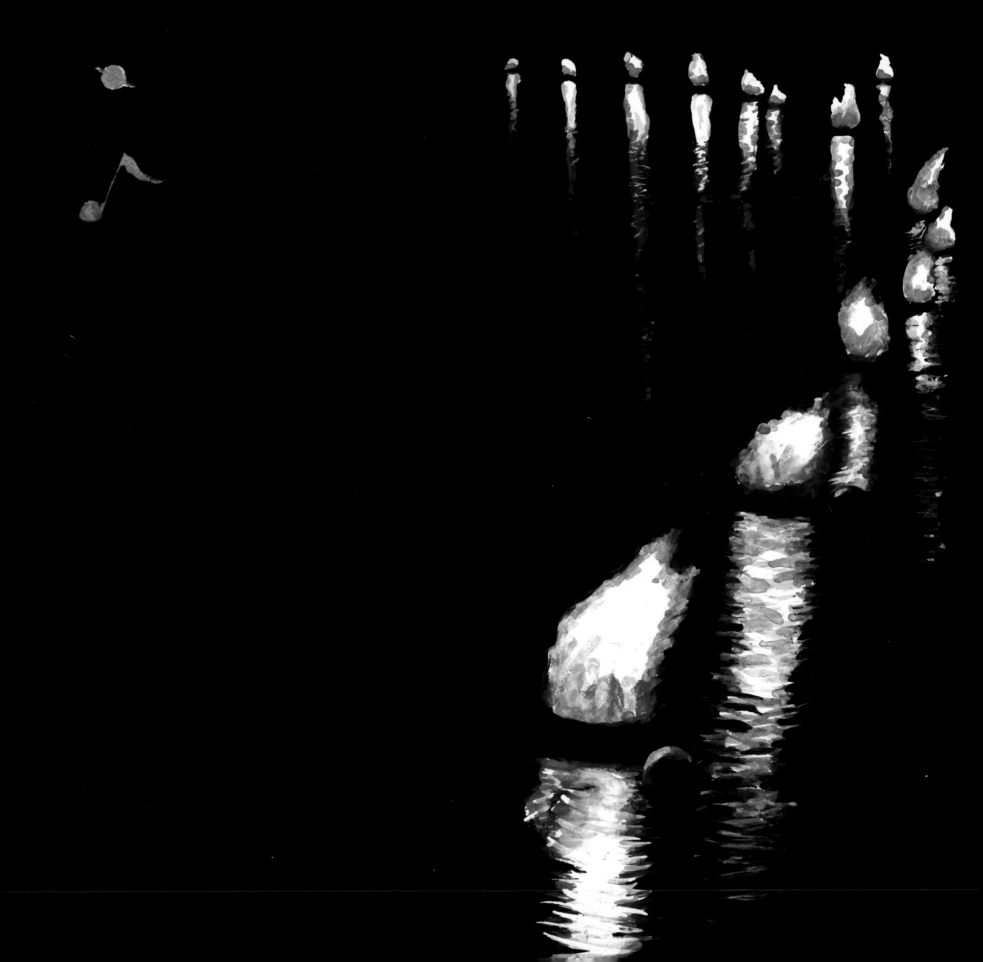

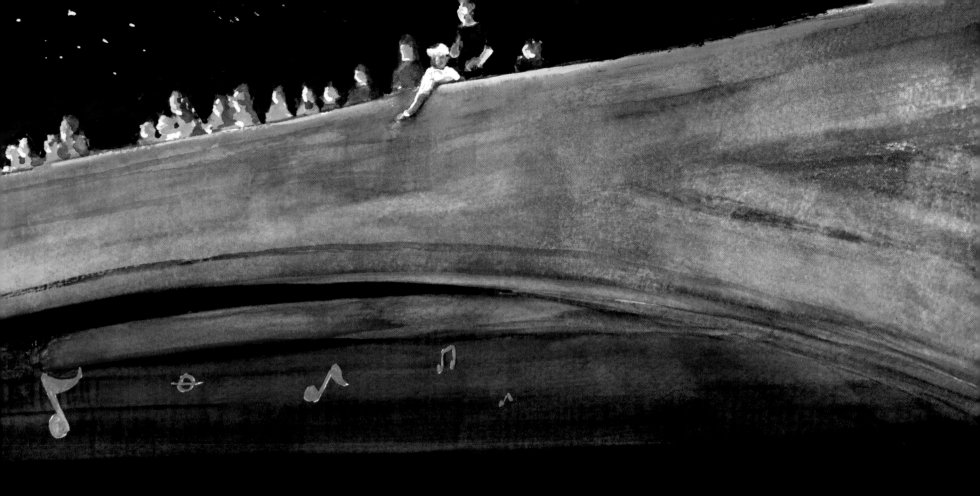

Now for the first time Little Duck looked up at the river banks
and saw all the people. They smiled and waved to Little Duck as she
paddled and danced along. Little Duck realized that they too had heard
and followed her song!

Above and beyond the people, Little Duck saw the tall buildings of the
city of Providence! A great blend of stone architecture from the past and
gleaming glass skyscrapers of the future, all caught in the dance of
the present. The sparks and sweet scent of wood smoke wafted upward
toward the night sky.

She turned and scooted away from a gleaming black gondola gracefully gliding by. Little Duck had never seen such a beautiful boat – long and sleek and shiny black, with firelight reflecting from bow to stern.

Then came a low dark boat filled with firewood for the fires. Carefully and quietly, the people in the boat fed the flames in time to the music. They slipped by Little Duck with a nod and a smile.

It was all so magical and lovely!

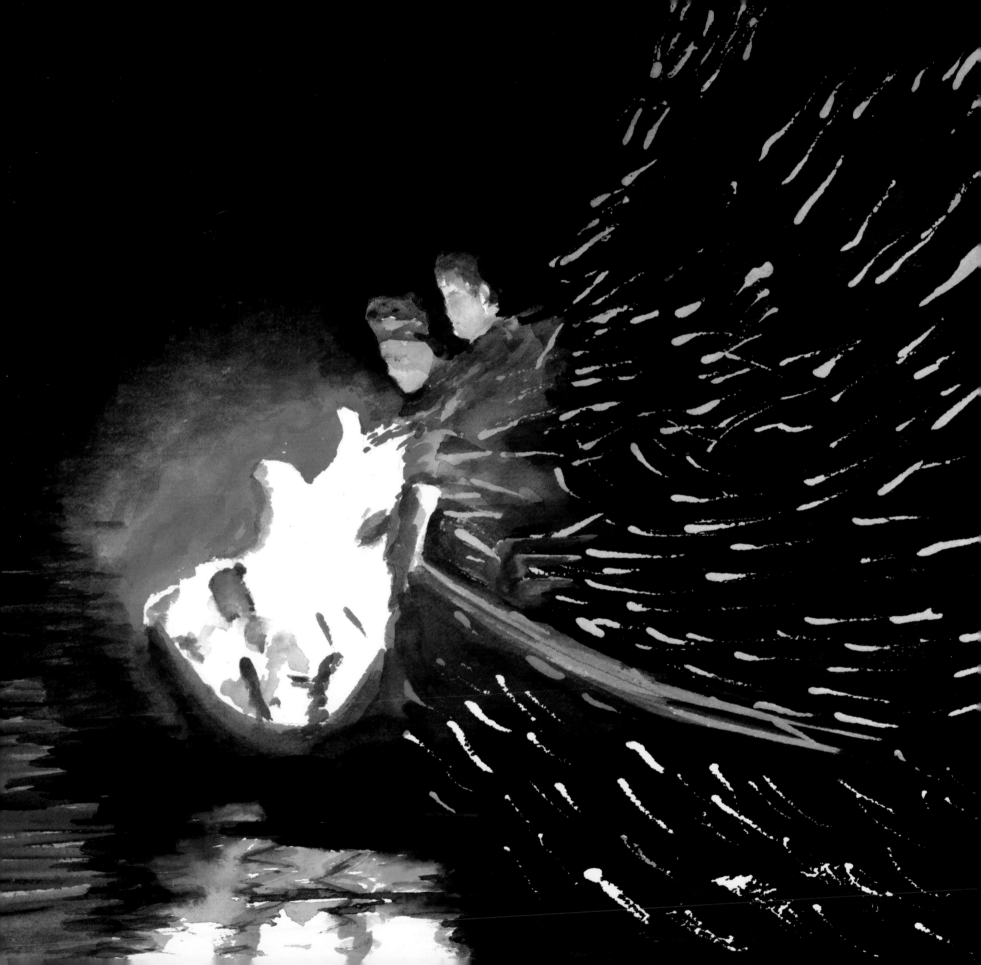

The people, the music, the fires, the sky, the deeply scented air –
all in the beautiful city of Providence! It was all so perfect!
So wonderfully perfect!

Little Duck swirled and twirled amidst the fires
and danced to the music with a happy rat-a-tat-tat!
Little Duck danced and danced all night long!

Little Duck was so happy that she
danced the next night and the next
and throughout the whole summer.
She danced through the last WaterFire
of the year when the flames lit the first
snowflakes, as they fell silently into the river.

Only then, when the last fires burned down to
deep orange embers and the final notes were echoes
in the wind, did Little Duck head home.

Rat-a-tat-tat! Next summer she would be back!

She hoped that all the world would hear her song and follow where it led:

"There's a place where the rivers meet the sea.
There's a city that waits for you and me.
Fires dance on the waters
And music fills the air –
Find it, find it, find it –
If you dare!"